# IT'S NOT THE 'JEWISH CHRISTMAS'

by Norman Geller

**Cover by Albert J. Tomlinson**
**Illustrations by Jane C. Gruchow**

# PREFACE

There are two holidays, both representative of major western religions that occur at about the same time of the year: Christmas and Chanukah. In areas where the population mix of Jew and Christian is fairly equal, this book could be extremely helpful in providing understanding. In areas of high Christian or Jewish density, this book could provide a primer of information concerning the existence and comparison of these observances, as well as the influences they bear on each other. Certainly, there is much more to both religious holidays than is outlined here.

This is a story that will, ideally, precipitate an extended dialogue. It represents not only an unusual friendship, but also a reflection of that natural curiosity and innocence associated with youth. The message and example could help lead to a world of increased respect for people's beliefs, feelings, and backgrounds.

It was a crisp October morning in New England. Jonathan was shuffling his way to school through the fallen leaves of the tree-lined streets. He loved watching his feet move through the autumn covering and often looked back to see the path he was making. He entered the school yard, looked around at the empty playground, and realized that he was late once again.

1

"I might be in trouble," he thought as he ran up the cement steps to the red brick schoolhouse. He rushed to his classroom and stopped for a moment to catch his breath. Knocking quietly, he opened the door and smiled at the teacher.

"Come in, Jonathan," she said. "I was just introducing our newest student—Samuel. He'll be sitting in the seat behind you, so why don't you show him where it is."

"Sure thing," Jonathan said with a sigh of relief.

During recess, Jonathan walked over to Samuel and said, "I'm glad you started school today. Otherwise, I might have been punished. The teacher gets upset when I'm late."

"Are you late often?" Samuel asked.

"I guess so. Say, where is your new home?"

"On South Side Road."

"That's where I live. Did your folks buy that big brown house?"

"Yes. Could we walk home together? I'm not sure of the way."

"We can walk together both ways. Maybe then, I won't be late."

"Deal," they both said.

The school bell rang, and they returned to class.

Walking back and forth to school every day was good for both of them. Samuel learned a lot about his new town, and Jonathan stopped being late for school. By the end of the week, they had become best friends.

Friday afternoon, Jonathan asked, "What are we doing tomorrow?"

"I'll be with my parents in the morning."

"Where are you going?"

"We're going to synagogue."

"Why?"

"Because we're Jewish, and it's our Sabbath. We go to services every Saturday. My folks want to meet the Rabbi and talk about membership in the congregation."

"I've been to lots of different churches, but I've never seen the inside of a synagogue. Could I go with you tomorrow?"

"Sure. We'll talk about it this evening. You and your parents are coming for supper. Friday evenings are really special at our house. It's the beginning of the Sabbath."

"When do you observe the Sabbath?"

"On Saturday, but all our holy days begin the night before."

"Our Sabbath is on Sunday."

"I know. I have lots of Christian friends. Are you Protestant or Catholic?"

"My mother is Protestant, and my father is Catholic. I guess that makes me a little bit of both. We go to worship every Sunday, but not always to the same church. I like seeing the different services. It would be nice to see how Jewish people pray."

When Jonathan and his parents arrived at Samuel's home, they could smell all sorts of good things cooking. Jonathan rang the bell, and Samuel opened the door. He had a grin on his face and a little cloth cap on his head.

"What's that?" Jonathan asked, pointing to Samuel's head.

"It's called a yamulka, and we wear it when we say prayers. Some Jewish men wear them all the time. My Dad and I are wearing them."

"May we wear them, too?" Jonathan's father asked.

"Sure," Samuel replied. "Come on in. I'll get them for you. Supper's almost ready."

Samuel's mother lit the Sabbath candles and quietly chanted a prayer. Her head was covered with a beautiful white lace shawl, and her arms moved around the flames as if she were drawing them near. Then, Samuel's father raised a shiny wine cup and chanted a prayer called "kiddush." On the table were two beautiful braided loaves of specially baked bread called "challah," and when the people sat down, another blessing was recited and a piece was given to everyone. Jonathan really enjoyed the Sabbath meal.

Samuel asked, "Would it be all right for Jonathan to come with us to synagogue tomorrow?"

"Of course," Samuel's father replied.

6

At synagogue on Saturday, Jonathan couldn't understand the Hebrew, but read the English in the prayer book and watched. After the service, the Rabbi spoke with them. He thought Samuel and Jonathan were brothers.

"He's my best friend," Samuel said proudly.

Many times over the next weeks, Jonathan went to synagogue with Samuel, and Samuel also went to church with Jonathan. Occasionally, they attended each other's religion classes.

It was the week following Thanksgiving, and the first snow of the season covered the town with a blanket of white. From the inside of his house, Jonathan watched the falling snow. He turned his face from the window and said to his father, "Can we buy our Christmas tree this evening? I always like getting our tree when it's snowing."

"We'll go after supper."

"May I ask Samuel and his parents if they would like to come with us?"

"Sure."

"I'll run over and ask them."

"Supper will be ready in a few minutes."

"I'll be right back."

Jonathan put on his hat, coat, and boots and went running out of the house. As he ran, he shuffled his feet through the snow to make a path. He often looked back at it and smiled.

Soon he was knocking on the door of Samuel's house.

"Hi, Jonathan. What do you think of this weather?"

"It's great! Maybe they'll call off school tomorrow. I can stay only for a minute. We're going Christmas tree shopping this evening. I thought we could all go together. You can buy your tree at the same time."

"We don't have a Christmas tree in our house. Did you forget that we're Jewish?"

"I thought everyone celebrates Christmas."

"We celebrate Chanukah."

"Is that the Jewish Christmas?"

Before Samuel could answer, the phone rang, and his mother called out, "If Jonathan is still here, tell him he's wanted at home."

"I'd better run," Jonathan said. "I'll call you after supper."

Jonathan hurried home, shuffling as he went.

Samuel walked into the kitchen. His parents were preparing supper.

"Jonathan asked us to go Christmas tree shopping this evening."

His father looked up.

"What did you tell him?"

"I told him we don't have a Christmas tree."

"And....."

"I told him we don't celebrate Christmas."

"And....."

"I told him we celebrate Chanukah."

"And....."

"I don't know what you're looking for, Dad."

"Did you tell him that we'd be happy to go?"

"Are we going to buy a Christmas tree?"

"No, but we can help them pick out theirs."

"What a great idea!" Samuel beamed. "I'll call and tell him."

As his parents looked at each other and smiled, Samuel ran into the den to call his friend."

The Christmas tree stand was filled with trees and wreaths. Christmas music was playing, and lights of every color were flashing. The falling snow, the flashing lights, the music, the smell of the freshly cut trees, and the friendliness and excitement of the people gave Samuel a special feeling. He said, "This is great. I never did anything like this before."

Jonathan smiled and said, "I'm glad you're here."

The snow that had been falling lightly became heavier and continued throughout the night. By the next morning, almost all activities in the town were cancelled.

The phone rang in Samuel's house. It was Jonathan.

"I want to learn about Chanukah. Why don't you and your parents come over and visit."

"I'm sure that will be all right," Samuel replied. "We'll see you in a little while."

Soon, all three of them were bundled up and walking towards Jonathan's house. When they arrived, they went into the family room where a cheery fire was blazing in the fireplace.

"Tell me about Chanukah," Jonathan said.

Samuel thought a moment and replied, "More than 2000 years ago, a brave band of soldiers called Maccabees fought to regain their house of worship, the Temple. After many long and hard battles, they finally won. Then they started to prepare the Temple for its rededication. Chanukah means 'dedication.' To do so, they had to light a flame that burned above the altar. They called that flame the 'Eternal Light' because it burned all the time. It used a special oil squeezed from olives, and it took about a week to prepare.

When they went to the cabinet where the oil was kept, they found all the bottles, except one, broken. That bottle of oil should have burned for only a day; but, instead, it burned for more than seven until a new supply was ready. It was said to be a miracle and that the Jewish people were to remember it every year.

"We do lots of things to celebrate the holiday, the most important being the lighting of a special nine branch candlestick called a menorah. We use one candle to light the others. We light one candle the first day, two the second, three the third, all the way to the eighth day when all the candles are burning. We add a candle a day because, with each day, the miracle became bigger. We eat special foods and play holiday games. It's really a fun time.

Samuel continued, "I've heard about Christmas. But, now I want you to tell me what it really means."

"It's the day when Jesus was born. We believe that He is the Son of God, and we are celebrating His birthday. Jesus was born in a manger because there was no room for His family at the inn. There was a special star in the sky to mark His arrival, and many people brought Him gifts. We also believe that He came to make the world a better place in which to live and that He will return some day. It's a good time to remember all those things He taught that can bring peace on earth and good will to everybody.

"We also have all kinds of holiday foods, decorations, and fun things. You know about Santa Claus, Rudolph the Red-nosed Reindeer, and The Little Drummer Boy. They all have a part in making Christmas very special."

Both families continued telling the stories and customs of the two holidays.

"Yesterday, I asked Samuel if Chanukah is the Jewish Christmas," Jonathan said.

Samuel's father answered, "No. It's not the Jewish Christmas any more than Christmas is the Christian Chanukah. Both holidays come at about the same time of the year, involve lights and decorations, are family holidays, and have become times for gift giving, especially to children. However, that's all they have in common. They are two different and separate religious observances. For the Jew, it is the remembrance of the miracle of the oil, and for the Christian, it is the birth of the Christ Child."

"Could Jewish people have a Christmas tree?" Jonathan asked.

"Of course they could. Who would stop them? However, we wouldn't."

"Why not?"

"When you look at your Christmas tree and wreath and nativity scene, do they remind you of something?"

"They remind me of Jesus, His birth, the Wise Men, and lots of other things."

"Exactly. To you, they are symbols of the holiday. To us, they would just be decorations. We don't think it is proper to take something that is holy for some people and use it only to make our house pretty."

"I never thought of it that way before. It really makes sense."

Samuel looked up and asked, "Why do we need so many religions in the world? Wouldn't it be easier if there was just one?"

Jonathan's father answered, "I don't know if it would be easier, and I'm not sure it would even be better. There are some people who believe in God and others who do not. It's important that we respect everybody, even those who don't believe exactly as we do. The most important thing is that people try to be good to each other and to themselves.

"Where we live, most of the people are either Protestant, Catholic, or Jewish; but, in the world, there are many, many different religions. They are all paths which lead to the same place, the belief and understanding of God. Which path we take is a matter of personal choice, and I suppose there could be as many paths as there are people who believe."

Samuel's father added, "We often talk about the two of you and your very unusual friendship. You really try to understand and respect each other. The more you learn about your religions, the more you will see how much they have in common. The symbols and practices might differ, but the basic beliefs are the same. Ask any leader of a major religion how many gods there are in the world, and the answer will always be the same, 'one.' There are many religions, but they all believe in one God, not my God, or your God, but one God.

"Now, look at the beautiful day that God gave you. You're not going to waste it by staying inside, are you?"

The two boys looked at each other and smiled.

Jonathan said, "Want to build a snowman?"

Samuel replied, "I'd rather build a fort and challenge the other kids."

"Let's do both," Jonathan grinned.

"Can I help you decorate your tree?" Samuel asked.

"Only if you show me how to light the menorah," Jonathan answered.

"Deal," they both said.

They put on their hats, coats, and boots and shuffled into the snow.

NER TAMID
ETERNAL LIGHT

HAPPY CHANUKAH

DREIDEL

MENORAH

JUDAH THE MACCABEE

MERRY CHRISTMAS

SANTA CLAUS

STAR OF BETHLEHEM

LITTLE DRUMMER BOY

THE THREE WISE MEN

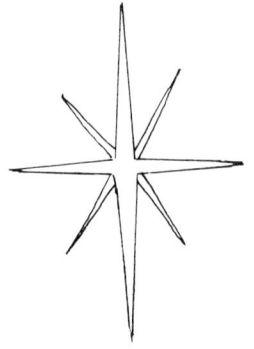

CHRISTMAS TREE

BABY JESUS